WRITING REPORTS ABOUT LITERATURE

COPYING MASTERS

ADVENTURES
for Readers: Book Two

PEGASUS EDITION

Harcourt Brace Jovanovich, Publishers

Orlando   San Diego   Chicago   Dallas

ACKNOWLEDGMENTS

Adapted from "Writing Exposition: Summaries and Reports" in *English Composition and Grammar,* Benchmark Edition, Second Course, by John E. Warriner. Copyright © 1988 by Harcourt Brace Jovanovich, Inc. Reprinted by permission of Harcourt Brace Jovanovich, Inc.

Front Cover: Landscape Window, Fenway Gate, Boston.
Stained glass by Tiffany Studios (c. 1912).
Photo: Alstair Duncan

Back Cover: Greak silver coin from the fourth century B.C.
Collection of Athena Blackorby
Photo: Benn Mitchell

Printed in the United States of America

ISBN 0-15-334983-2

CONTENTS

ON THE USE OF *WRITING REPORTS ABOUT LITERATURE*

As your students study literature, you may require them to write research reports about selections they have read in *Adventures for Readers: Book Two,* Pegasus Edition. Writing a report is a complex task, one for which students may require special instructions and guidance. For this reason, the *Teacher's Literature Companion: A ResourceBank* includes a booklet entitled *Writing Reports About Literature*. The pages in the booklet, which are blackline copying masters that you may duplicate and distribute in your classroom, provide suggestions students can follow to develop reports about literature.

Each writing activity discussed in this booklet builds upon the previous activity in such a way that students are gradually led to write a research report on a literary topic. The first activity requires students to summarize a piece of literature. Students are shown how to take notes and organize information so that it is appropriate to their purpose and audience. In addition, they are given specific guidelines for writing and evaluating and two sample summaries to use as models. The second activity has students write a book report. This activity uses what students have already learned about writing summaries and shows them how to combine a selective summary with their impressions of a work's literary value. As before, students are given a model to examine and guidelines for evaluating to use when revising their own book reports.

The third and final activity prepares students to write a research report on a literary topic. The booklet helps students develop their reports by following the stages of the writing process: prewriting, writing, evaluating and revising, proofreading, and preparing a final verson. In the **prewriting** section, students are shown how to read a literary work carefully, develop a topic; begin research, develop a preliminary thesis statement and outline, take notes and evaluate and revise the preliminary thesis statement. Sample source cards and note cards are included as models for students to follow. In addition, sections labeled "Before You Write" summarize or highlight important points students should consider during the prewriting stage. The section on **writing** gives students guidelines for writing the first draft of the research report. In the section on **evaluating** and **revising,** students learn how to identify the strengths and weaknesses of their drafts and how to make changes to improve them. The discussion of evaluating includes a set of questions entitled "Guidelines for Evaluating Reports on Literary Topics." Students can ask themselves these questions to identify specific aspects of their drafts that require revision; and, if you wish, you may use the guidelines as criteria for evaluating and asssigning a grade to the students' final reports. The booklet concludes with a sample research report on Langston Hughes's early interest in literature and writing.

Depending on your students' needs and abilities, you may want to duplicate and distribute the booklet in its entirety, or you may choose to distribute the booklet in sections, as students work on a particular stage of the writing process.

Writing Reports About Literature

As you continue your study of literature, you will respond to what you've read in a variety of ways. You will often share your reading experiences and ideas with others through discussions and through writing. When you write about topics concerning literature, there are several ways you can develop ideas or present information.

WRITING SUMMARIES OF LITERATURE

A **summary** is an account in your own words of a longer piece of writing. When you write about literature, you will often find it useful to summarize the details of a story, novel, poem, or play. As with other forms of writing, preparing a summary involves using the writing process.

CONSIDERING PURPOSE AND AUDIENCE

Your purpose may be to inform your audience of the literature's content so that they can decide whether they wish to read it, too. For example, you and your classmates may participate in a short-story exchange. If you do, each class member would read a different story and would briefly summarize its contents. Then, these individual story summaries would be gathered into a class book. Other members of the class could review the collected summaries to find stories that sound appealing to them. You might, for example, tell your readers that your story was a

mystery, but you would not want to give away the story's ending.

On the other hand, you may summarize information from a piece of literature in order to support an idea or opinion you have developed about what you have read. Imagine that you and your classmates have just finished reading a play. The class is divided: half the class members think the play's main character is sensitive, and half do not. You decide to support your opinion in writing. Your purpose is to explain your opinion to your classmates by summarizing details about the character that support your point of view. Your audience has read the play, but a summary of selected details or events may refresh their memories or help them to see things in a new way.

GATHERING INFORMATION

The first step in writing a summary of a piece of literature is always to get an overview by carefully reading the entire piece. During this first reading, do not take notes. Instead, concentrate on understanding what you read. After you have finished, go back through the piece again. This time, jot down the main ideas. In taking notes, be certain that you use your own words.

If you are writing to inform your reader about the literature's content, first identify the piece's title and author. You may also wish to identify the literature by its form (short story, novel, play, poem) or type (Western, mystery, romance, etc.). Include details about the story's time, place, main characters, and conflict. Notice how these details appear in the example on the following page.

EXAMPLE

Original Piece of Literature

"The No-Talent Kid," found on pages 10–20
Adventures for Readers: Book Two

Notes

1. "The No-Talent Kid" by Kurt Vonnegut—short story
2. *Time*—fall, beginning of school and marching band season
3. *Place*—a high school known for its award-winning marching bands
4. *Main Characters*—Mr. Helmholtz, band director
   —Walter Plummer, a bad but earnest clarinet player for C Band
5. *Conflicts*—Mr. Holmholtz wants an eight-foot bass drum for his A band but has no money.
   —Walter Plummer wants a position in the A Band but does not have enough musical talent.

Notice that the writer of these notes concentrates on background information about the story and on outlining the story's main conflicts. The notes do not include specific details such as the short scene that takes place in Mr. Helmholtz's house.

If you are writing to explain an idea, clearly identify it. Then include only the details that are directly related to your main point. Notice the details in the following example:

EXAMPLE

Original Piece of Literature

"The No-Talent Kid," found on pages 10–20 of *Adventures for Readers: Book Two*

Notes

Main Point: Walter Plummer is resourceful in achieving his goals.

1. Walter is in C Band but wants to be in A Band.
2. Walter buys a new clarinet, which he hopes will improve his playing ability.
3. Walter challenges a member of the A band for his position.

4. Walter tries to work his way into the band by buying an eight-foot bass drum and fulfilling Mr. Helmholtz's dream.
5. Walter and Mr. Helmholtz negotiate a deal concerning the drum.
6. Walter gets a position in the A Band.

Notice that the writer of these notes focuses upon Walter's resourcefulness. The specific details identify Walter's goal and include all the ways in which he tried to achieve it. Notice that the notes primarily summarize Walter's part in the story and do not include many details about Mr. Helmholtz.

Before You Write. Carefully consider what information you will include when you summarize a literary work.

- Think about these questions:
  1. What is my purpose in summarizing the work? Do I want to inform about the content or to explain an idea?
  2. What are the most important details about this work? If I am writing to inform, what type of literature is it? Where and when does the story (book, play) take place? Who are the main characters? What is the main conflict?
  3. What supporting details (minor characters, events, or descriptions) can be left out of the summary without changing the essential meaning?

- Do not rely on your memory for correct spellings of characters' names and details. Always check the literary work for such information.

- As you take notes, remember to:
  1. Follow the order of events as they occur in the literary work.
  2. Put ideas and events into your own words.

WRITING THE FIRST DRAFT

Rely primarily on your notes to write the first draft of your summary. Add specific details that relate directly to your points, but keep your summary brief and focused on your main point. Remember, your readers are reading your summary to preview a piece of literature or to learn more about your ideas. They are not interested in an involved retelling of the story. For all the details, they can read the original literary work. As you read the examples beginning on the following page, notice how the writer's purpose determines what details are included.

EXAMPLE

Original Piece of Literature

"The No-Talent Kid" found on pages 10–20 in *Adventures for Readers: Book Two*

Summary to Inform

"The No-Talent Kid," a fictional story by Kurt Vonnegut, is set in a high school in the fall just as classes resume. The school is known for its award-winning bands. As the story begins, the bands are organizing for marching season. The two main characters are Mr. Helmholtz, the school's band director, and Walter Plummer, a tone-deaf clarinetist returning for his third year in the C Band (the lowest band). Mr. Helmholtz desperately wants to obtain an eight-foot bass drum so that his top band, the A Band, can recover its recently lost position as the top band in the state. However, a lack of funds makes his wish seem impossible. Walter Plummer desperately wants to be a member of the A Band so that he can earn a school letter sweater. His lack of musical talent makes fulfillment of his wish seem impossible. The story concerns both characters' attempts to turn their wishes into realities. Mr. Helmholtz tries but fails to buy an eight-foot bass drum from a bankrupt organization. Walter Plummer challenges the first chair clarinet player in the A Band and ends up in the last chair, or position, in C Band. Both goals seem impossible to obtain. How each character finally achieves what he wants makes an interesting conclusion to the story.

Summary to Explain an Idea

Walter Plummer, one of the main characters in Kurt Vonnegut's short story "The No-Talent Kid," has no musical talent. Nevertheless, it is clear from the story's action that Walter is resourceful. In his third year in the high-school's C Band the (lowest-level), Walter seems to have little chance of achieving his goal and becoming a member of the A Band (the top level). He has tried all the usual methods to gain success. He has bought a new clarinet. He has challenged a member of the A Band to capture his position, but nothing works. However, after a conversation with his band director, Mr. Helmholtz, Walter figures out another way to become a member of the A Band. If he cannot get in on musical talent, maybe he can get in by fulfilling Mr. Helmholtz's dearest dream and getting an eight-foot bass drum for the band. In one evening, Walter contacts a bankrupt organization that happens to own an eight-foot bass drum, sells his new clarinet, and buys the drum. The next day during A Band's practice, Walter appears with the drum. With some skillful bargaining and talking on both characters' parts, each ends up with what he really wants. Mr. Helmholtz gets the bass drum for his band, and Walter wins a position in the A Band. By not giving up and by trying some unusual methods, Walter demonstrates his resourcefulness and ultimately achieves his goal.

When You Write. While writing your summary, follow these guidelines:

- State the piece of literature's main points clearly and briefly.
- Present the main points in a clear order, usually following the order presented in the original piece of literature.
- Keep your summary short.

EVALUATING AND REVISING

Like any other first draft, the first draft of your summary can probably be improved. When you examine a first draft to locate its strong points and weak points, you are evaluating your work. If possible, put your first draft aside for several hours or a day before you evaluate it. Then reread your first draft, and answer each of the questions in the following guidelines.

GUIDELINES FOR EVALUATING A SUMMARY

Main Ideas	Are only the main points of the literary work included in the summary?
Audience	Is the summary suitable for the audience?
Paraphrasing	Is the summary written in the writer's own words?
Order	Are the main points in the summary presented in a clear order?
Length	Is the summary short, usually no more than a paragraph?

After you have evaluated your summary, revise it by using the four basic revision techniques: **adding, cutting, reordering,** and **replacing**. Always refer directly to the literature you are summarizing when you add or replace details. Proofread your revised summary to locate and correct any errors in grammar, usage, and mechanics. Then make a final copy according to your teacher's directions. Proofread again to catch any errors made in recopying.

WRITING A BOOK REPORT

A book report gives two kinds of information: what the book is about and what you think of it. When you tell what the book is about, you need to use your summarizing skills. When you explain what you think about the book, you need to present your opinions and specific details from the book to support those opinions.

PREWRITING HINTS FOR WRITING A BOOK REPORT

As with other types of writing, it is important to consider the purpose and audience for your book report. You will also need to gather specific information from your book.

The purpose of writing a book report is to inform your audience about the book's content and about your opinion of the book. In the first part of a book report, you usually tell what the book is about, identify the title and author, and explain whether the book is fiction or nonfiction. If you are reporting on a novel, indicate the background of the story—time, place, main characters, and conflict. For a nonfiction book, summarize the important information given. If you are reporting on a biography, indicate why the person written about is important, and mention chief incidents in that person's life.

In the second part of a book report, you usually explain your reaction to the book. This part of the report is important because it shows how carefully and thoughtfully you have read the book.

Before You Write. Whether you liked or disliked the book, ask yourself specific questions concerning your reactions:

- Were the characters interesting and believable, or were they boring and unbelievable?
- Was there a strong plot, or was it predictable?
- Did the book deal with important issues? Was it pure escapism? Was it entertaining?

- Did you learn new or important information?
- Was the book easy to read or was it a struggle to get through?

Answering questions like these will help you to think of specific reasons for your reaction to the book. These specific reasons will also help your readers to decide whether the book appeals to them.

Use specific details or examples from the book. Whether you are telling about the book's content or your reaction to it, support what you say with specific details or examples from the book. You may want to quote words or sentences from the book. If you do, be sure to enclose these direct quotations with quotation marks.

As you gather specific details, keep your audience and purpose in mind. Your audience wants to learn whether they would enjoy reading this book. To help your audience make an intelligent decision, provide background information without giving away crucial details of the plot, give specific reasons for your opinion of the book, and support your reasons with specific examples.

In preparing a book report, use the note-taking skills that you developed in summary writing. After you read the book, jot down notes about its content and your reaction. Look up details that you may have forgotten about the plot and the characters.

Summarize information about the book. Avoid getting bogged down in too many details. Your purpose is not to rewrite the book. You cannot possibly give every detail of plot in a novel or every piece of information in a nonfiction book, nor do you want to. Remember your purpose is to inform others about the book's content so that they can decide whether to read the book themselves. Concentrate on selecting important details about the plot and the main characters, or discuss the main ideas in a nonfiction book.

WRITING

After you have finished gathering ideas and details for your report, write a first draft. In preparation for writing your own report, read the sample report that begins on the following page. As you read the example, ask yourself these questions:

1. What is the book about?
2. What specific details does the writer give about its content?
3. What is the writer's reaction to the book?
4. What specific details are included to support the writer's reaction?

A Report on <u>The Martian Chronicles</u>
by Ray Bradbury

   <u>The Martian Chronicles</u> is Ray Bradbury's science-fiction novel. It covers the years 1999–2026 when Americans have first traveled to and colonized Mars. Part of the action takes place on earth but most takes place on Mars. As Bradbury sees it, Mars is not an uninhabited, dry planet when the first American explorers arrive there. Instead, it is populated by Martians who enjoy a highly developed civilization and culture. There are conflicts between the Martians and the ''invading'' Americans and among the Americans on earth and on Mars. These provide the action for Bradbury's story.

   I like this book because it gives an interesting glimpse into one man's view of what the future may be like. For example, in one chapter Bradbury describes a ''typical'' American house of 2026 that is programmed to run itself. Breakfast is cooked and the dishes are cleared and cleaned automatically. Tiny robot mice are in charge of cleaning the entire house. Also, even though we now know that there is not life on Mars, in the future we could discover a civilization like Bradbury's Martians who communicate through mind reading and read books by simply passing their hands over the pages.

   Another reason I like <u>The Martian Chronicles</u> is that each chapter of the book contains a complete story. Of course, some characters appear in more than one chapter. Also, the book as a whole tells the story of the American colonization of Mars, but each chapter has a point and its own conclusion. Some chapters tell funny stories, such as when Mars is temporarily depopulated. Only a few Americans are left. One man and one woman accidentally find out about each other's existence. Before this discovery, each had thought he or she was the only one left. At first they are overjoyed to find company. Then they find out that they aren't a good match at all. Other chapters are more serious and deal with important issues, such as what happens when one culture ignores another instead of understanding or learning from it. Still other chapters focus on the feelings of both the Americans and the Martians. For example, in one chapter, a lonely, older couple whose son has died on earth retires on Mars. By using his mental powers, a lonely Martian takes on the form of their dead son.

The Martian Chronicles is a very entertaining story that held my interest. At the same time, it raises important questions. Will Americans repeat their past mistakes in the future? What would be the effects of a worldwide nuclear war? Reading this book makes readers like me more aware of these questions so that we can try to search for better answers.

EVALUATING AND REVISING

After you have completed a draft of your book report, take time to evaluate and revise it. The following guidelines will help you identify the strengths and weaknesses of your draft. Always try to set your draft aside for a while before evaluating and revising it so that you can examine it from a fresh, objective point of view.

GUIDELINES FOR EVALUATING A BOOK REPORT

Title, Author	Are the book's title and author mentioned early in the report? Is the title of the book underlined when it is mentioned?
Content, Reaction	Does the report give information about both the book's content and the writer's reaction to the book?
Development	Do specific details and examples support the writer's statements about the book? Do specific reasons explain the writer's reaction to the book?
Novel	For a novel, are the setting and main characters discussed? Is enough of the plot revealed to give readers a general idea of the story?
Nonfiction	For a nonfiction book, does the report summarize important information?

As you revise, keep your evaluation in mind. Use the four basic revision techniques: **adding, cutting, reordering,** and **replacing**. For example, add specific details to support your points or to strengthen your audience's understanding of the story. Delete any details that do not relate specifically to your point.

After revising for content, you should proofread your report to locate and correct any errors in grammar, usage, and mechanics. Make a final copy according to your teacher's directions. Then proofread again to catch any errors or omissions made in recopying.

WRITING A REPORT ON A LITERATURE TOPIC

As you continue to read and explore literature, you may have questions about the author or the work. You may enjoy certain authors and wonder how and when they began to write or what they were like when they were your age. You may wonder if experiences in the authors' lives contributed to what they wrote or how they wrote it. You may wonder about what else certain authors have written. You may even wonder what other readers' reactions have been to a piece of literature. Finding answers to these questions requires that you gather and organize information from a number of sources. To write a report on a literary topic, follow these basic steps:

1. Develop a limited topic
2. Gather information
3. Organize the information
4. Write a first draft
5. Evaluate and revise the report

DEVELOPING A LIMITED TOPIC

Sometimes your teacher will assign a specific report topic about literature; at other times you may be asked to develop your own topic. If you begin with a broad subject, such as an author, a work or a literary period or movement, you must limit it in the same way you would limit a composition topic. Remember that you can limit a broad subject by analyzing it—dividing it into its parts.

Before You Write. Think about what makes a topic suitable for a report about literature.

- A suitable topic is not too broad to be developed well in several paragraphs.
- A suitable topic is not too narrow. Very narrow topics make it difficult or impossible to find information in the library that fits the topic.

- A suitable topic requires research. It cannot be fully understood simply by reading the literary work. Your report will probably be a short one, perhaps only several paragraphs long. The topic should be one about which you can give detailed information in that amount of space.

- The purpose of a report about literature is to present information. Select a topic about which you can find information in sources such as books and encyclopedias, not a topic based on personal experience. For example, you may have had an exciting experience as a cast member in a production of *The Diary of Anne Frank*. Your experience is a personal one; you will not find information about it in your library. However, you could write a report about some aspect of the play—how audiences and critics responded to it when it was first produced, or how the play differs from the original book and why these changes were made. You would be able to find needed information for these topics in the library.

- The topic you develop should also be interesting to your audience. Most audiences are interested in new or unusual topics or in fresh information on well-known topics. For example, your classmates have probably read some of William Shakespeare's poetry. They may not know, however, that many of his poems were written for a "mysterious, dark lady" or that many of Shakespeare's poems follow a pattern so well identified with him that it now bears his name.

Before You Write. Choose a limited topic to develop in your report.

- Preview selected material on your topic. Read a specialized reference article or look over the index or table of contents of any book on your subject to limit the broad subject to a narrow topic. Asking yourself questions about the subject and its parts may also help you to identify your writing focus.

- Think about your audience and their interests when you develop a limited topic: What do they already know about the subject? What aspect, or part, of the subject will be new to them?

- Keep in mind both the number of available sources and the length of your report. A short report on a subject with many sources means limiting your subject more than you would for a longer report or a report based on fewer sources.

- Remember that the main purpose of a report is to present information you have gathered.

Avoid limited topics for which you would rely on your own experiences or opinions. A topic such as "why *Shane* is a great western story" is better suited for a book report than for a report on a literary topic.

Here is an example of developing a limited topic from a broad subject. Notice how each step involves dividing the broad subject into smaller and smaller parts.

1. Black writers (broad subject)
2. Langston Hughes (one black writer)
3. The life of Langston Hughes (one aspect of this writer)
4. Langston Hughes's early experiences with reading and writing (limited topic—one aspect of his life)

The last step is a suitable topic. First, it treats only one aspect of Hughes's life, so it is not too broad. Second, the topic is not too narrow. Because Langston Hughes was a well-known black writer, information about him would not be difficult to find in the library. Finally, the topic requires research. You could not just read one of Hughes's poems to write a report about his early experiences with reading and writing.

GATHERING INFORMATION

The reference section of your library is the best place to begin gathering information. An encyclopedia or other general reference work will often provide a good introduction to your topic. However, this introduction is usually only a general one. For a topic dealing with literature, you may also find additional information in more specialized reference books such as the *Something about the Author* series, the *Contemporary Literary Criticism* series, the *American Women Writers* series, *The Science Fiction Encyclopedia*, and the *Literary History of the United States*.

EXAMPLE

Before You Write. Locate sources of information on your topic.

- Write down the titles of any sources listed at the end of encyclopedia articles about your topic. Look for these sources in your library.
- Look under all possible subject headings in the card catalog and the *Readers' Guide to Periodical Literature*. Sources with information on Langston Hughes, for example, might be found under "Hughes, Langston," "The Harlem Renaissance," and "Black Writers."
- Check the bibliography (an alphabetical list of sources the author used) in any useful book you find to identify other possible sources.
- Examine both the index (an alphabetical list of topics covered in that book) and the table of contents (a list of chapter titles) to find how much information that source has about your topic.

Record information about the sources from which you gather information. Your readers will want to know where you found the information used in your report. They also may want to read more about your topic or to check that you have reported information accurately. When you take notes from a source, prepare a separate card, called a *source card*, that gives information about the source.

Use 3 × 5-inch note cards or slips of paper as source cards. The source cards you prepare for books, magazine articles, and encyclopedia entries will be slightly different. On the source card for each, record the following information.

An encylopedia or reference book source card:

1. The name of the author of the article, if there is one
2. The name of the article (in quotation marks)
3. The name of the encyclopedia or reference book (underlined)
4. The year of the edition

"Hughes, (James) Langston."
Something about the Author.
1983 ed.

①

Sample index card

Notice the punctuation in the sample card above. A period comes at the end of the article's title, before the quotation marks. A period also follows the name of the encyclopedia. Note that *edition* is abbreviated as *ed.*

A book source card:

1. The name of the author (last name first)
2. The title of the book (underlined)
3. The place of publication
4. The name of the publishing company and the year of publication

EXAMPLE

> Meltzer, Milton. *Langston Hughes: A Biography.*
>
> New York: Thomas Y. Crowell Co., 1968.
>
> ②

Sample index card

Place a comma between the author's first and last names. A period comes after the author's name and after the book's title. Notice the colon after the place of publication and the comma between the name of the publishing company and the year of publication.

A magazine or newspaper source card:

1. The name of the author, if there is one
2. The name of the article (in quotation marks)
3. The name of the magazine or newspaper (underlined)
4. The date of the magazine or newpaper
5. The page numbers of the article

EXAMPLE

> Wertz, Irma Jackson. "Profile: Langston Hughes." *Negro History Bulletin* Mar. 1964: 146 – 47.
>
> ③

Sample index card

If the article begins on one page and then continues later in the magazine, put a comma between page numbers. A hyphen between page numbers means that the article is on all pages between the numbers. The date is written day (if given), month, year, with a colon following the year. Also notice that neither the word *page* nor its abbreviation *p.* is used and that a period follows the page number. The months of the year—except May, June, and July—are abbreviated.

Note that each source card has a circled number in its upper right-hand corner. As you fill out each source card, assign a number in this way to each

source. Later, when you begin taking notes, you can mark each note card with this number, instead of writing out the name of the source on each note card.

DEVELOPING A WORKING OUTLINE

As you read about your topic, develop a working outline. Suppose you are preparing a report on Langston Hughes's early experiences with reading and writing.

In the library, you may have found a reference article, two books, and a magazine article about your topic. After reading the reference article, you decide that you will deal with the following three main points or ideas in your report.

I. Hughes's early experiences with reading

II. Hughes's early experiences with writing

III. Hughes's decision to become a writer

These points are the beginning of a working outline that can guide your research. You now know, for example, that you need to find information on each of these three points. You may discover other ideas as your research continues. If a new idea seems important to your report, add it to your rough outline. If you are gathering many notes on one point, consider breaking that heading down into two or more subdivisions.

EXAMPLE

Sample index card

The number in the upper right-hand corner of the sample note card on the previous page means this note is from source card 2 (*Langston Hughes: A Biography*). Use separate note cards for each heading and for each source. For example, the note on the previous page is about stories Hughes heard from his grandmother. You might also find information on that idea in a reference book and a magazine article. You would then have three note cards with the same heading but with different source numbers.

Before you begin taking notes, read over your source material, looking for main ideas. Then, as you read over your material, jot down notes. There are three ways that you can take notes, illustrated in the examples below.

1. You can *paraphrase*, putting material in your own words.

2. You can *summarize* by giving only the main ideas.

3. You can *combine* paraphrasing with direct quotations from the material.

TAKING NOTES

Your reading will include reference articles, parts of books, and magazine articles. You cannot hope to remember all of the details of information that you collect. Consequently, you will need to take notes.

The best way to take notes is to write them on note cards or slips of paper, using a different card for each note. Early in your reading, you will find that information for your report falls under a number of general divisions or points. Once you have three or four divisions, you can use them as headings for your note cards. When you find information that relates to one of these headings, write the heading at the top of the card and underline it. Then write your notes under the heading. Underneath the note, write the page number(s) on which you found the information.

Original

> I was the Class Poet. It happened like this. They had elected all the class officers, but there was no one in our class who looked like a poet, or had ever written a poem. There were two Negro children in the class, myself and a girl. In America most white people think, of course, that *all* Negroes can sing and dance, and have a sense of rhythm. So my classmates, knowing that a poem had to have rhythm, elected me unanimously—thinking, no doubt, that I had some, being a Negro.
> Langston Hughes, *The Big Sea*

Paraphrase of information

> Hughes was elected Class Poet. All the other class officers had been elected. No one in his graduating

class had any experience or qualifications for the position. Hughes and another child were the only blacks in class. Hughes's white classmates believed the old stereotype that all blacks have a sense of rhythm and knew a poem also needed rhythm. His classmates elected Hughes unanimously for the position based upon the following logic: All blacks have a sense of rhythm; Hughes is black; Hughes must have a sense of rhythm.

Summary of information

Hughes was elected Class Poet. He was one of two blacks in the class—the rest of the class was white. Hughes's white classmates believed the old stereotype that all blacks have a sense of rhythm. Since poems need rhythm, Hughes could provide it.

Paraphrase of information, with quotation

Hughes was elected Class Poet. All the other class officers had been elected, but Hughes said, ''there was no one in our class who looked like a poet, or had even written a poem.'' Hughes and another child were the only blacks in class. His white classmates believed the old stereotype that all blacks have a sense of rhythm and knew a poem also needed rhythm. His classmates elected Hughes unanimously for the position based upon the following logic: All blacks have a sense of rhythm; Hughes is black; Hughes must have a sense of rhythm.

ORGANIZING THE REPORT

Now you must prepare to use the notes for your report. Eliminate notes that contain duplicate information or facts that do not fit into your limited topic. Next, sort the cards into piles according to their headings. Each pile will contain all the information on one main idea or point. Review each pile to decide if you have enough notes to explain each heading, or if you should gather more. Also, decide if a large number of notes should be divided into two headings.

After eliminating and sorting, you are ready to shape your final outline. Put your headings and

subheadings in a logical order that will make sense to your audience. Then prepare a final outline, using correct outline form. Study the following final outline for a report on Langston Hughes. Notice how it is both similar to and different from the working outline.

I. Early experiences reading and listening to stories with others
    A. Mother
    B. Grandmother
II. Early experiences with reading by himself
    A. Grade school reading
    B. High school reading
III. Early writing of poetry
    A. Grammar School Class Poet
    B. High School Class Poet
IV. Early writing of prose
    A. "Mary Winosky"
    B. Wish to write like de Maupassant
V. First published piece and decision to become a writer
    A. "A Negro Speaks of Rivers"
    B. Career disagreements with father

WRITING THE FIRST DRAFT

As you write the first draft of your report, consider the following suggestions.

1. Remember that a report about literature is a kind of expository composition. As such, it has the same basic parts: *introduction, body, conclusion.* It should have an interesting, limited topic sufficiently developed with specific details.

2. Be certain that you understand all the terms you use. Look up difficult or unfamiliar words in the dictionary.

3. Use your own words in writing the report. Introduce quotations only when they are particularly apt or striking, and use them correctly. Copy the writer's exact words, if you use a direct quotation. Enclose the writer's words in quotation marks, and give the page number on which the quotation appears.

4. Put every necessary detail into your report, and omit unnecessary items. Stick to your topic.

5. Using your outline as a guide, present information in a logical order, one that is easy for readers to follow.

At the end of your report, list the sources for your material. Study the list of sources at the end of the model report that begins on page 14.

Notice that sources are listed alphabetically by the last name of the author; if an author is not given, the source is listed alphabetically by the first word in the title.

If you filled out your source cards correctly, making a list of your sources is easy. You can copy information directly from these source cards. However, before you begin, check each source card to be sure you have (a) included all the required information for that source (b) recorded information in the right order, (c) recorded all information accurately, and (d) used punctuation correctly.

EVALUATING AND REVISING YOUR REPORT

If possible, put your first draft aside for a few days. This time away from your writing will help you look at it more objectively. To evaluate your report, either alone or in a small group, carefully examine your first draft. Decide how well it meets the guidelines for a report about a literary topic. As your reread your first draft, ask yourself each of the questions in the following Guidelines for Evaluating Reports on Literary Topics. Your answers to these questions will help you decide where you need to make changes in, or to revise, your first draft.

GUIDELINES FOR EVALUATING REPORTS ON LITERARY TOPICS

Topic	Does the report have a suitably limited topic? Is it suitable for the audience?
Introduction	Does the introduction catch the audience's attention?
Paragraph Development	Does each paragraph have a main idea expressed in a topic sentence? Is this main idea developed with details?
Conclusion	Does the conclusion signal that the report is ending, without repeating ideas in the body?
Unity	Are all details in the report related to the topic?
Order	Are details given in a logical order?
Topic Development	Does the report include enough information to develop the topic?
Source Material	Is the report written in the writer's own words? Is the material paraphrased or summarized as appropriate? Does quoted material use quotation marks for the writer's exact words?
Sources	Are sources listed at the end of the report?

After you evaluate your draft, you can revise it by using the four basic revision techniques: **adding, cutting, reordering,** and **replacing**. Once you make changes to improve your draft, you should proofread it to locate and correct errors in grammar, usage, and mechanics. Then make a final copy by following your teacher's directions. Proofread again to catch any errors or omissions made in recopying.

ANALYZING A MODEL

You use the critical thinking skill of *analysis* when you look closely at something to understand what its parts are and how they are put together. Carefully examining the parts and organization of a model report on a literary topic will help you write your report. As you read the model beginning on the following page, notice how the writer introduces the topic and develops it further in each paragraph. Think about the writer's plan of organization, whether paragraphs are arranged in a logical order, and look for topic sentences in each paragraph. Also proofread the model. Has the writer overlooked any errors or weaknesses in grammar, usage, or punctuation? Are all words spelled correctly, including proper capitalization? Finally, examine

Finally, examine the writer's list of sources on page 18. Is all information given in the correct order and form? Are the cited works punctuated properly?

After you have analyzed the model, think about it. Was it interesting and informative? What parts or sentences did you find particularly well written? Were any parts or sentences unclear? Do you think that the writer's use of questions in the introduction was effective? Why, or why not? How well did the writer fit the research into the report? Do facts seem to fit naturally, or do they seem "tacked on"? How well did the writer bring the report to a close in the conclusion?

When you write your own reports, always be sure to analyze them carefully, following these guidelines and the others given on the preceding pages.

Langston Hughes: Early Interests in Literature and Writing

Langston Hughes wrote poetry, plays, short stories, novels, essays, song lyrics, two autobiographies, and nonfiction. With so much writing to his credit, did this famous author grow up always knowing that he would become a writer? Was there a definite turning point in his life? What were his early experiences with books and stories? Who were his favorite authors when he was growing up? When did he first begin to write? Finding answers to these questions can give us insights into Langston Hughes, the man and the writer.

Both his mother and his grandmother gave Langston Hughes important early experiences with books and stories. His mother, who wrote poems herself, read to Langston before he learned to read. She took him to visit the library in Topeka, Kansas, where they lived and to see plays such as <u>Uncle Tom's Cabin</u> and <u>Under Two Flags</u>. When he was in second grade, Langston Hughes went to live with his grandmother in Lawrence, Kansas. She read the Bible aloud to him. As they sat on the front porch of her home, his grandmother also told Langston Hughes many stories. These were about his own family members and about important champions of black freedom such as John Brown, Frederick Douglass, David Walker, Nat Turner, and Harriet Tubman. As Hughes grew older, she shared the magazine <u>Crisis</u>, published by the NAACP, with him and read aloud from W. E. B. DuBois's <u>The Souls of Blackfolk</u>.

Quite soon after he learned to read, books became an important part of Langston Hughes's life. After he went to live with his grandmother, he was quite lonely. To escape from his loneliness, he often entered into the world of books. There he found happy solutions to problems that he did not always find in real life. In grade school, Langston Hughes enjoyed reading westerns by Harold Bell Wright and Zane Grey. Although he was not particularly interested in poetry in grade school, he did enjoy Longfellow's Hiawatha and Paul Lawrence Dunbar's poetry, written in black dialect with a definite swing and beat. Later, in high school, Langston Hughes especially enjoyed the fiction of Edna Ferber, Theodore Dreiser, and Guy de Maupassant. His high school English teacher introduced him to the "controversial" new poets of the time, such as Vachel Lindsay, Amy Lowell, Robert Frost, and Carl Sandburg. Langston Hughes especially liked Carl Sandburg's poetry. He liked Sandburg's use of free verse, language, and images, and he identified with the midwestern subjects of Sandburg's work.

Langston Hughes wrote his first poem after he was elected Class Poet of his eighth grade graduating class in Lincoln, Illinois. According to Hughes's own account, no one in his class had ever written a poem, but they needed a class poet for graduation exercise. Langston Hughes and another girl were the only blacks in the class. Believing the stereotype that all blacks have rhythm, his classmates chose Langston Hughes as Class Poet. In response, Hughes wrote a sixteen-verse poem, one of the longest of his career. Eight verses praised the school's eight teachers, and eight verses praised the graduating class. The poem was a great success when Hughes read it on graduation night.

Langston Hughes was also elected Class Poet of his high school graduating class. This time, however, his classmates had strong reasons for selecting him. Langston Hughes attended Cleveland

Central High School, where he published many poems in the school's magazine, the <u>Belfry Owl</u>. During these years, Hughes said poems seemed to come almost spontaneously to him. His high school teachers encouraged his writing, and he kept a separate notebook for his poetry.

Although he wrote a great deal of poetry in high school, Langston Hughes did not write much prose. As a class assignment, he wrote "Mary Winosky," a short story about a white, immigrant scrubwoman. The idea for this story came from a small newspaper article that Hughes had read. He recalled that he had no stories in his mind at this time, but one important high school experience did foreshadow the short stories that he was to write much later. Taking French, Langston Hughes struggled to translate and understand the writings of Guy de Maupassant. One evening, the beauty of de Maupassant's expression and use of language seemed to break through to him. This experience made Hughes want to write stories about blacks that would have truth and meaning for people everywhere in the world regardless of their nationality and background.

It was shortly after his graduation from high school that Langston Hughes had his first poetry published. Graduating from high school in 1920, Hughes took a train south from Cleveland, Ohio, to Mexico to visit his father. As his train crossed the Mississippi River, Hughes's personal thoughts and feelings combined with his study of history and geography. His poem "A Negro Speaks of Rivers" flowed quickly from his mind onto an old envelope. Later, in Mexico, he sent it off to New York City to <u>Crisis</u>, the same magazine he had read with his grandmother years earlier. <u>Crisis</u> ran "A Negro Speaks of Rivers" in its June, 1921 edition, and Langston Hughes at the age of nineteen, was in print for an adult audience.

It was also during this yearlong visit to his father in Mexico that Langston Hughes made his career decision. Hughes's father wanted to send his son to college. However, he wanted Langston to study in Switzerland to become a mining engineer. This plan did not appeal at all to Hughes who did not enjoy mathematics or physics. In discussions with his father, Hughes realized for the first time not only what he did not want to do with life, but what he did want to do with it. He wanted to become a writer.

In 1921, Langston Hughes's forty-six year writing career was just beginning, but many important elements for his success were already in place. His mother, his grandmother, his classmates, his teachers, his reading, and his experiences had all combined with his natural talent to put him on his way to a career in writing.

Sources

"Hughes, (James) Langston." <u>Something about the Author</u>. 1983
    ed.

Hughes, Langston. <u>The Big Sea</u>. New York and Wang, 1940.

Meltzer, Milton. <u>Langston Hughes: A Biography</u>. New York:
    Thomas Y. Crowell Co., 1968.

Wertz, Irma Jackson. "Profile: Langston Hughes." <u>Negro History</u>
    <u>Bulletin</u> Mar. 1964: 146–47.

A 8
B 9
C 0
D 1
E 2
F 3
G 4
H 5
I 6
J 7